W9-BRT-717

LOCKS, CROCS, & SKEETERS

The Story of the Panama Canal

by Nancy Winslow Parker

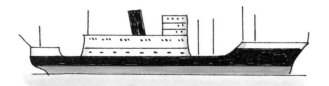

 GREENWILLOW BOOKS   NEW YORK

This book is dedicated to John and Helka Gordon,
Atle and Carol Gjelsvik, and Sally Swift, whose help
and encouragement made the passage through
the Panama Canal a voyage of wonder and joy.

Grateful acknowledgment is made to Nan S. Chong, Canal Collection Library, Balboa,
Panama; Louis Sorkin, M.S., Department of Entomology, The American Museum
of Natural History, New York; Nancy Treacy, Ocean County Library, Point Pleasant,
New Jersey; and Skip Lester, Mantoloking, New Jersey.

Black pen, watercolor paints, and
colored pencils were used for the
full-color art. The text type is
Bookman BT.

Printed in Hong Kong by South China
Printing Company (1988) Ltd.

First Edition
10 9 8 7 6 5 4 3 2 1

Library of Congress Cataloging-in-Publication Data

Parker, Nancy Winslow.
Lock, crocs, and skeeters: the story of the Panama
Canal / by Nancy Winslow Parker.
   p.   cm.
ISBN 0-688-12241-8
1. Panama Canal (Panama)—History—Juvenile
literature.   2. Panama—History—Juvenile
literature.   3. Americans—Panama—Panama
Canal—History—Juvenile literature.   I. Title.
F1569.C2P37   1996   972.87'5—dc20
95-17845   CIP   AC

PART I

"BEYOND THE CHAGRES"

*A Poem About
the Isthmus of Panama*

BY JAMES STANLEY GILBERT

Beyond the Chagres River
    Are paths that lead to death—
To the fever's deadly breezes,
    To malaria's poisonous breath!

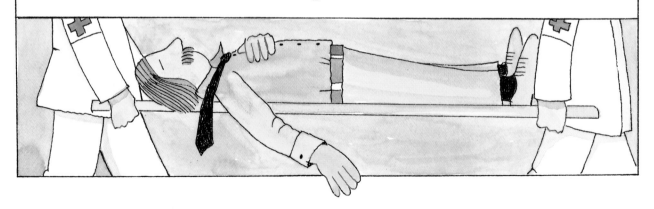

Beyond the tropic foliage,
Where the alligator waits,
Are the mansions of the Devil—
His original estates!

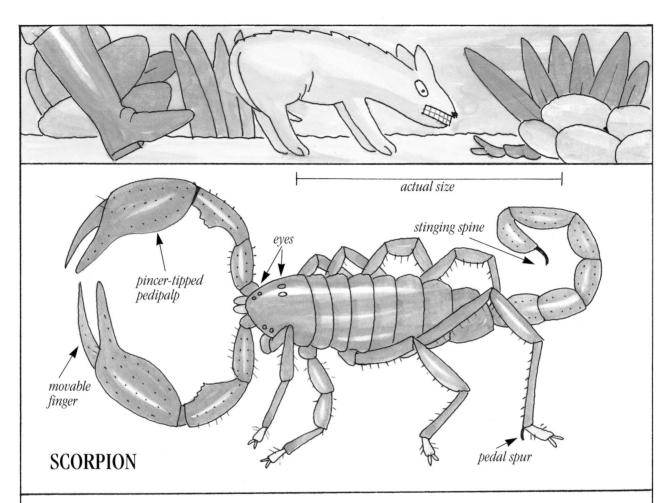

SCORPION

actual size

pincer-tipped pedipalp

eyes

stinging spine

movable finger

pedal spur

Beyond the Chagres River
Are paths fore'er unknown,
With a spider 'neath each pebble,
A scorpion 'neath each stone.

'Tis here the boa-constrictor
  His fatal banquet holds,
And to his slimy bosom
  His hapless guest enfolds!

Beyond the Chagres River
Lurks the cougar in his lair,
And ten hundred thousand dangers
Hide in the noxious air.

Behind the trembling leaflets
Beneath the fallen reeds,
Are ever-present perils
Of a million different breeds!

Beyond the Chagres River
　　'Tis said—the story's old—
Are paths that lead to mountains
　　Of purest virgin gold!

But 'tis my firm conviction
Whatever tales they tell,
That beyond the Chagres River
All paths lead straight to hell!

JAMES STANLEY GILBERT

AMERICAN POET

James Stanley Gilbert was one of the few people to write about life in tropical Panama. He was born in Middletown, Connecticut, and educated at the Skinner School in Chicago. After graduation he worked as a cashier and book-keeper. In 1886 he went to Panama and worked for several years in the commissary department of the Panama Railroad Company at Cristóbal. He later became a partner in a steamship agency representing, among others, the United Fruit Company. Gilbert was described by a British diplomat friend as "a man who lived lustily as men did in those times when life in the tropics meant death hovering around the corner."

Gilbert had begun to write poetry about Panama while employed as a shipping agent, and he continued to do so for the rest of his life. From "Away down south in the Torrid Zone," the first line of his first poem, readers were captivated by Gilbert's vision of the tropical pre-canal Panama. His poems in *Panama Patchwork*, the book in which "Beyond the Chagres" appeared, were called "documents of life on the Isthmus" by a *New York Times* reviewer in 1906. His fans called him the "poet laureate of the Isthmus of Panama" and compared him to Rudyard Kipling. But the double life of businessman-poet did not please his critics, who thought he should spend more time improving his poems.

Gilbert never lived to see the Panamanian jungle tamed and its diseases conquered, or the opening of the Panama Canal. He died on August 15, 1906, in the Colón hospital, a victim of "yellow eyes," his nickname for the deadly malaria. He is buried in Mount Hope Cemetery, the old "Monkey Hill," just outside the city of Colón, Isthmus of Panama.

PART II
THE STORY OF THE PANAMA CANAL

"THE EIGHTH WONDER OF THE WORLD"

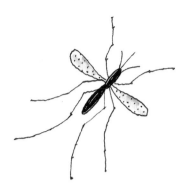

THE ISTHMUS OF PANAMA

For at least 400 years people dreamed about digging a canal across the Isthmus of Panama, a skinny strip of mosquito-infested jungle measuring 37 miles wide by 480 miles long in Central America. It is the narrowest strip of land in the Western Hemisphere. For ships sailing from New York to San Francisco, or the other way around, the canal would cut 7,800 miles. It would eliminate the long and dangerous sea journey around South America and Cape Horn, the terror of seamen. A canal would save weeks, if not months, of travel.

But none of the dreamers could foresee the horrible suffering, disease, death, and failures that would befall those who tried to change Panama's Chagres, the "River of Crocodiles," into a canal that would carry ships from ocean to ocean.

The first dreamer was King Charles V of Spain. In 1534 his soldiers had to struggle across the Isthmus on a bumpy stone road, El Camino Real, with the stolen riches of Bolivia and Peru piled on the backs of mules and horses. The road went from Panama City on the Pacific to Nombre de Dios and later Portobelo on the

Caribbean, where the gold and silver were loaded onto ships and carried across the sea to Spain.

About 300 years later, in 1849, gold was discovered in California. Fortune seekers swarmed across the Isthmus by mule, by canoe, and on foot to Panama City, where they could board sailing ships for San Francisco. By 1855, despite many deaths from malaria and yellow fever, an American company succeeded in completing a railroad across the Isthmus to transport the prospectors and their families.

day in what was at that time one of the worst pestholes on earth. Gilbert had seen the workers stricken with malaria, yellow fever, bubonic plague, and alcoholism, and watched the daily trains carrying bodies to the cemetery on nearby Monkey Hill.

Americans came to Panama in 1904 to take up the challenge of building a canal. They were well aware of the problems on the Isthmus, and they made two important decisions. The first was to get rid of the mosquitoes in order to reduce disease. The second was

In 1882 the French began digging a great trench—*la Grande Tranchée*—across the Isthmus. It had been the dream of Ferdinand de Lesseps, but his canal company ultimately collapsed because of disease, corruption, and mismanagement. In 1889 the French abandoned the partially excavated canal, leaving costly dredges, steam shovels, derricks, and buildings to be swallowed up by the Panamanian jungle.

James Stanley Gilbert's poems are about life on the Isthmus. He lived there during the French effort to build a canal and the first years of the American canal-building effort. His poem "Beyond the Chagres" documents some of the horrors the workers faced every

to build a lock-and-lake canal, not a sea-level canal as the French had tried to do. There was just too much water on the Isthmus for a sea-level canal. With a lock-and-lake canal, the flooding of the Chagres River during the rainy season and the drainage of the water along the Isthmus could be controlled by a dam, and the tidal variations of the Pacific Ocean could be accommodated.

It took the Americans ten years of hard work and the involvement of diplomats, engineers, scientists, steel and cement manufacturers, and thousands of pick-and-shovel workers before the dream could be realized. In 1914 the Panama Canal was opened to ships from any country in the world.

VASCO NÚÑEZ DE BALBOA
SPANISH EXPLORER

Vasco Núñez de Balboa came from Xerez de los Caballeros, a town in Spain. Encouraged by stories of wealth to be made in the newly discovered world, he packed his bags and at the age of 26 sailed across the sea in search of fame and fortune. He landed in what is now Haiti on the island of Hispaniola, the main Spanish base, where he raised pigs. Consumed by ambition, he then stowed away on a ship (in a barrel!) bound for the mainland.

On the Isthmus of Darien (today's Panama) Balboa founded a colony. Friendly Indians told him of a vast body of water beyond the mountains, so he set out with 190 Spaniards and several hundred Indians to find it. It took the expedition 25 days of marching through dense jungle to cover 45 miles.

On September 25, 1513, the Spaniards arrived at the summit of a mountain. Balboa advanced alone to behold the vast unknown ocean, which he named the Great South Sea (later renamed the Pacific Ocean). Four days later the expedition reached the water. Balboa waded in with naked sword raised in one hand and the royal banner in the other and proclaimed that the sea and all the land it touched belonged to the king of Spain. When Balboa returned to Hispaniola, he expected to be greeted as a hero. Instead the new governor, Pedro Arias de Ávila, known as Pedrarias, who was jealous of Balboa's fame, falsely accused him of treason. Balboa was beheaded in 1519.

Today the monetary unit of Panama is the balboa. A portrait of Balboa in high-crested helmet and armor appears on several of the coins. The paper currency is the U.S. dollar, which Panamanians also call the balboa.

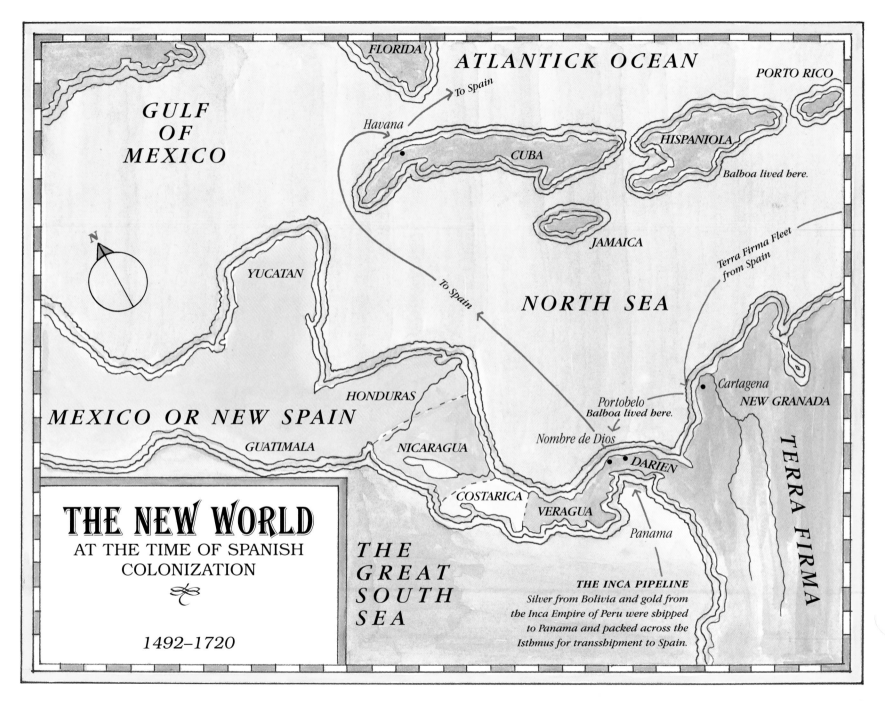

FLORIDA

ATLANTICK OCEAN

PORTO RICO

GULF OF MEXICO

To Spain

Havana

CUBA

HISPANIOLA

Balboa lived here.

JAMAICA

N

Terra Firma Fleet from Spain

To Spain

NORTH SEA

YUCATAN

Cartagena

HONDURAS

NEW GRANADA

MEXICO OR NEW SPAIN

Portobelo
Balboa lived here.

GUATIMALA

NICARAGUA

Nombre de Dios

•DARIEN

TERRA FIRMA

COSTARICA

VERAGUA

Panama

THE NEW WORLD

AT THE TIME OF SPANISH
COLONIZATION

❦

1492–1720

THE GREAT SOUTH SEA

THE INCA PIPELINE
*Silver from Bolivia and gold from
the Inca Empire of Peru were shipped
to Panama and packed across the
Isthmus for transshipment to Spain.*

FERDINAND DE LESSEPS
FRENCH DIPLOMAT AND CANAL BUILDER

Ferdinand de Lesseps came from a distinguished French family. He was born in 1805 in Versailles, and followed his family's tradition of government service, holding posts as a diplomat in Europe and North Africa. While on duty in Cairo, he realized how useful it would be to have a canal running from the Red Sea to the Mediterranean Sea. When his diplomatic career ended, he approached the ruling pasha of Egypt with a plan for such a canal, received the consent of the Egyptian government, and went to work organizing the construction. Fifteen years later, in 1869, the Suez Canal was completed. Its opening received worldwide attention, and de Lesseps was proclaimed a hero and great canal builder.

Encouraged by that success, de Lesseps, now known as the Great Frenchman, turned his thoughts to the Isthmus of Panama and to the digging of a sea-level canal from ocean to ocean. He formed the Compagnie Universelle du Canal Interocéanique de Panama as a private venture, sold shares in it, and bought the rights to the Isthmus from its owner, Colombia. He hired the finest engineers in France to begin construction in 1881. But he underestimated the enormous problems of the venture.

Corruption in Paris, mismanagement of the company, and the severe climate and diseases of the Isthmus brought de Lesseps's efforts to an end in 1889. Thousands of French investors lost their life savings.

De Lesseps was accused of fraud, and there was a sensational trial in France. He was convicted and almost went to jail, but his sentence was reversed on appeal. He died in France at the age of 89.

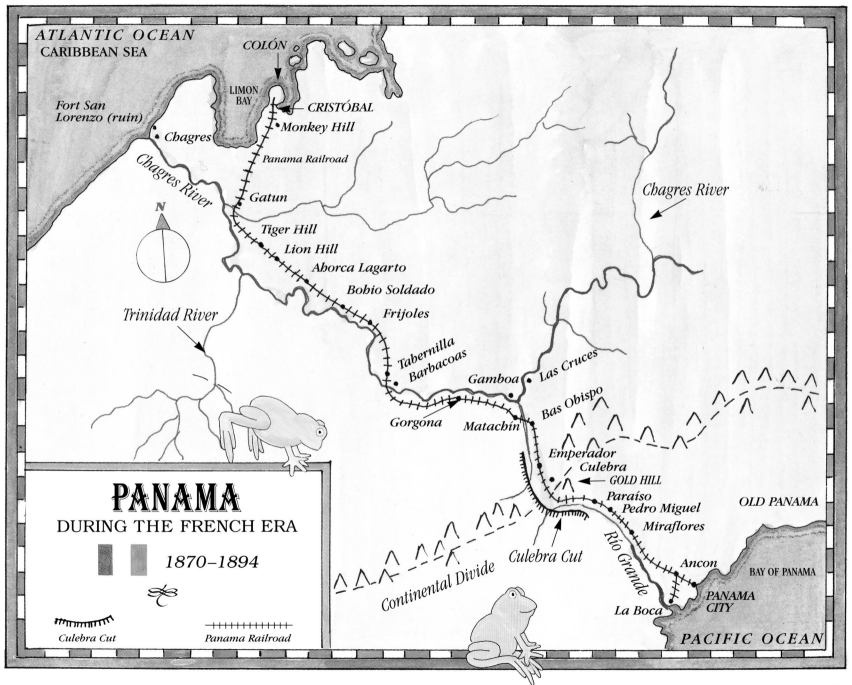

ATLANTIC OCEAN
CARIBBEAN SEA

COLÓN

LIMON BAY

Fort San Lorenzo (ruin)

CRISTÓBAL

Chagres

Monkey Hill

Panama Railroad

Chagres River

Gatun

N

Tiger Hill

Chagres River

Lion Hill

Ahorca Lagarto

Bohio Soldado

Trinidad River

Frijoles

Tabernilla
Barbacoas

Gamboa

Las Cruces

Gorgona

Matachin

Bas Obispo

Emperador
Culebra

GOLD HILL

OLD PANAMA

PANAMA
DURING THE FRENCH ERA
1870–1894

Culebra Cut

Continental Divide

Paraíso

Pedro Miguel

Miraflores

Río Grande

Ancon

BAY OF PANAMA

La Boca

PANAMA
CITY

Culebra Cut

Panama Railroad

PACIFIC OCEAN

President Roosevelt at the controls of a 95-ton Bucyrus steam shovel in Pedro Miguel, Canal Zone, 1906

THEODORE ROOSEVELT

29TH PRESIDENT OF THE UNITED STATES

Theodore Roosevelt was born of wealthy parents in New York City and held many important positions before becoming president in 1901. He believed that a canal across the Isthmus of Panama was vital to the interests of the United States.

During his administration the United States agreed to buy the bankrupt (and renamed) Compagnie Nouvelle du Canal de Panama from the French and made a treaty with Colombia that gave the United States the right to build a canal across Panama. The Colombian Congress, however, delayed in ratifying the treaty, and Roosevelt became enraged, believing that "those bandits in Bogotá" were trying to extort undeserved millions from the French, another party to the treaty. When the Panamanians revolted against Colombia, Roosevelt supported them with gunboats and troops.

The revolt was successful, and in 1903 a treaty was signed between the new Republic of Panama and the United States that created the U.S. Canal Zone and gave the United States the right to build a canal. Colombia was furious, diplomatic fur flew, and Pan-American relations were destroyed for decades. Roosevelt admitted in a speech in 1911 at the University of California, Berkeley, ". . . I took the Isthmus, started the canal, and then left Congress not to debate the canal, but to debate me. . . . But while the debate goes on the canal does too."

Roosevelt visited Panama in 1906 and ate with the workers at a mess hall in La Boca. He had soup, beef, potatoes, peas, beets, chili con carne, plum pudding, and coffee. Roosevelt never returned to Panama and therefore never saw the completed canal. He died on January 6, 1919.

John Stevens and George Washington Goethals

CHIEF ENGINEERS

Much of the credit for the American effort in building a lock-and-lake canal in Panama goes to John Stevens, the chief engineer appointed in 1905. Stevens was born on a farm in Maine and spent years building railroads from the swamps of Minnesota to the deserts of New Mexico. He viewed the Panama project as simply dirt to be moved by the railroad. But mindful of the French failure, he ordered his chief sanitation officer, Colonel William C. Gorgas, to clean up Panama and eradicate the mosquitoes that carried yellow fever and malaria before any worker would be allowed to lift a pick or shovel. Stevens also organized the difficult technical engineering that was to come. Then, after one year and three months on the job, he quit, never explaining why.

The next chief engineer, appointed in 1907, was George Washington Goethals. Goethals was from a poor immigrant family. He worked his way through college and was graduated from the U.S. Military Academy at West Point. It was Colonel Goethals who commanded the digging of the canal, a U.S. government project under army supervision. To achieve the final extraordinary objective, he was given absolute power over everybody and everything in the Canal Zone, directing the operation of steam shovels, locomotives, track shifters, pile drivers, dredges, steamboats, and tugs and overseeing the dynamite crews and thousands of laborers. Goethals stayed with the job till its completion and achieved one of the most gigantic engineering feats in history: a canal where dams, locks, lakes, and railroad blend together into one harmonious operation.

On August 15, 1914, the canal was opened and the steamer *Ancon*, a cement boat, sailed quietly through.

Stevens   Goethals

WILLIAM CRAWFORD GORGAS
COLONEL, U.S. ARMY

The canal could never have been built without the efforts of William C. Gorgas and his army of mosquito fighters. Gorgas, the son of a Confederate general, was born in Mobile, Alabama. After medical school he enlisted in the army. Several posts later he was sent to Havana, Cuba, where he served under Dr. Walter Reed. In Cuba Reed proved that yellow fever is transmitted by the bite of a mosquito. Gorgas, his chief sanitation officer, was ordered to clean up Havana, street by street, house by house, to eliminate the pools of water where mosquitoes breed. Cases of yellow fever went from 1,400 in 1900 to zero in 1902.

In 1904 Colonel Gorgas, now a well-known mosquito specialist, was sent to Panama, which was a "mosquito paradise" with mosquitoes everywhere. To clean up the Isthmus, Gorgas was allowed all the laborers he needed. Among the supplies he ordered from the United States were huge amounts of wire screening; tons of pyrethrum powder, sulfur, and sulfur powder; gallons of kerosene, carbolic acid, wood alcohol, and mercurial chloride; thousands of garbage cans, buckets, brooms, scrub brushes; pounds of common soap; plus lawn mowers, fumigation pots, rat traps, padlocks, lanterns, and machetes.

Gorgas installed lids on rain barrels, drained ditches, spread oil on swamps, hauled away garbage, and destroyed rats, whose fleas could cause bubonic plague. He had screens placed on all doors and windows. At the end of two years the last case of yellow fever in Panama was reported, and cases of malaria greatly decreased.

Gorgas collecting *Anopheles* larvae and pupae from swamps along the canal line

YELLOW FEVER MOSQUITO

Aedes aegypti

There are 5,000 known species of mosquitoes, and they are found all over the world. The yellow fever mosquito, *Aedes aegypti*, is one of the world's most dangerous insects. It is a beautiful creature that lives in places with hot climates, such as Central and South America, Africa, and tropical islands. It breeds only in clean, fresh water or brackish water in artificial containers. The water must be near human habitation because the female mosquitoes feed on human blood (they love ankles!) and need blood meals to mature their eggs. The males drink only fruit juices and are harmless.

When a female *Aedes* bites a human, it takes blood and leaves a virus, the virus that causes yellow fever. Yellow fever is a disease that damages body tissues and the liver. On the 3rd or 4th day after the bite, the victim's skin turns yellow. Between the 5th day and the 8th day, the victim may die. But if the victim survives eight days, he or she will live and have lifelong immunity to yellow fever. Although there is now a vaccine to prevent yellow fever, 2 to 5 percent of its victims still die.

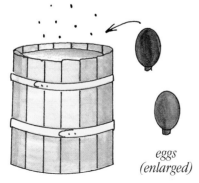

eggs
(enlarged)

rain barrel with clean or
brackish water near house

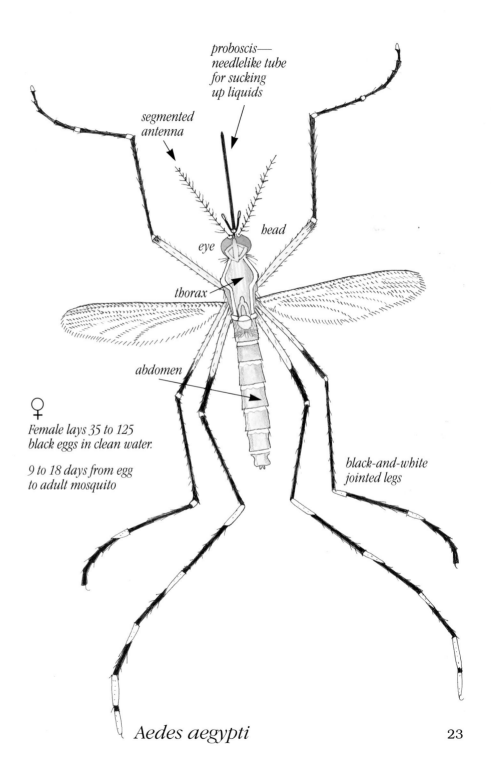

*proboscis—
needlelike tube
for sucking
up liquids*

*segmented
antenna*

head

eye

thorax

abdomen

♀
*Female lays 35 to 125
black eggs in clean water.*

*9 to 18 days from egg
to adult mosquito*

*black-and-white
jointed legs*

Aedes aegypti

23

MALARIA-CARRYING MOSQUITO

Anopheles albimanus

Anopheles mosquitoes are found all over the world in places with hot climates. There are over 300 species of *Anopheles*, and of these, 50 are major carriers of human malaria, a dangerous parasitic disease that kills 1 to 2 million people each year worldwide. One of the dangerous species is *Anopheles albimanus*, a large brown mosquito that thrives in steamy, humid Panama.

The life span of an *Anopheles* is 21 days. It breeds in clean or stagnant water in such places as marshes, lakes, puddles, and ditches, even in cows' hoofprints.

The males drink fruit juices and do not bite. The females spread malaria from person to person by extracting blood from humans who have malaria. The bites leave no swelling and no itch. When a mosquito swallows blood containing the malaria parasite (*Plasmodium falciparum*), the parasite travels to the mosquito's stomach and then to its salivary gland. The next time the mosquito bites someone, the now-infected saliva is shot into that unlucky person, who will contract malaria.

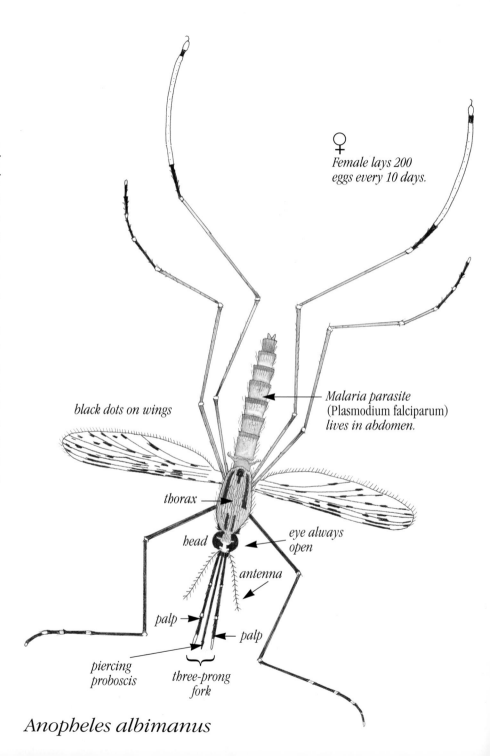

♀
Female lays 200 eggs every 10 days.

black dots on wings

Malaria parasite (Plasmodium falciparum) lives in abdomen.

thorax

eye always open

head

antenna

palp

palp

piercing proboscis

three-prong fork

Anopheles albimanus

THE COSTS OF THE CANAL

West Indian worker applying mosquito control larvicide, Miraflores, Canal Zone, 1910

The creation of the Panama Canal, from the first shovelful of mosquito-laden swamp to the quiet passage of ships through placid tropical waters, was a very expensive undertaking in both lives and dollars.

The cost in lives was staggering. It is conservatively estimated that in 1850, during the building of the railroad, more than 6,000 workers died, many of them Chinese and Irish. They died from smallpox, cholera, dysentery, fever, and malaria. Suicide claimed hundreds more.

During the French era, from 1881 to 1889, 22,000 workers died. Most of them were black Jamaicans who were victims of yellow fever, malaria, typhoid fever, smallpox, pneumonia, dysentery, beriberi, food poisoning, snakebite, and sunstroke. The French director general, Jules Isidore Dingler, lost his wife, son, daughter, and daughter's fiancé all within one year to yellow fever.

During the United States era, from 1904 to 1914, workers came from all over the world, but none came from China or Jamaica because of past unpleasant experiences on the Isthmus. In those ten years 4,500 black workers—mostly West Indians from Martinique, Barbados, and Guadeloupe—and 350 white workers died.

The total cost in dollars to build the canal was enormous: $287 million spent by the French and almost $400 million by the United States (more than was spent to buy the whole Louisiana Territory).

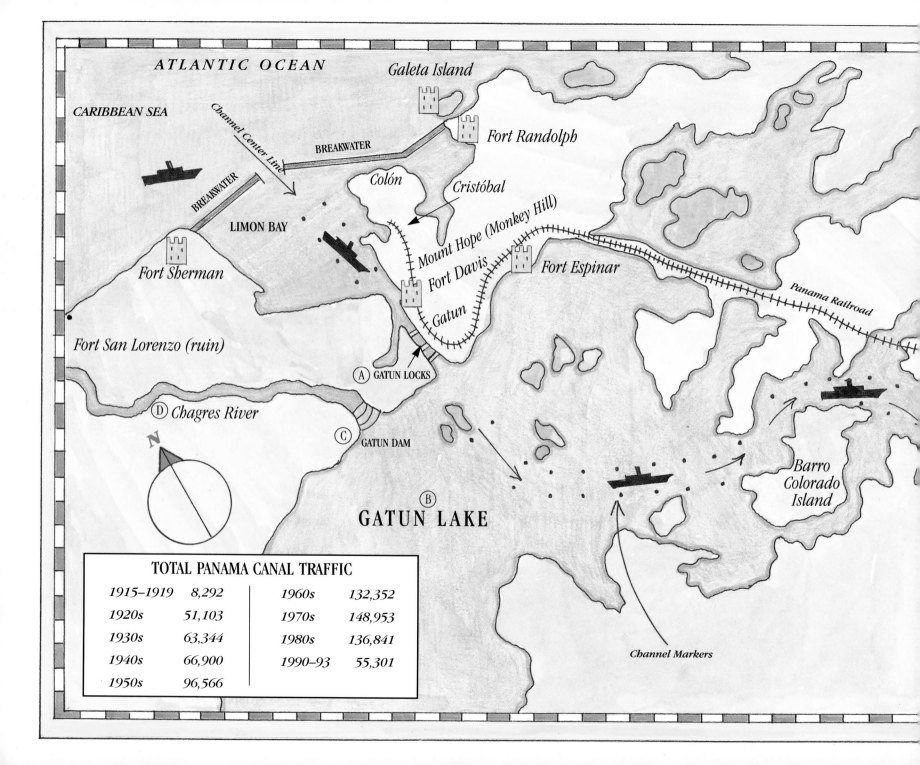

ATLANTIC OCEAN

Galeta Island

CARIBBEAN SEA

Channel Center Line

BREAKWATER

Fort Randolph

BREAKWATER

Colón

Cristóbal

LIMON BAY

Mount Hope (Monkey Hill)

Fort Davis

Fort Espinar

Panama Railroad

Fort Sherman

Gatun

Fort San Lorenzo (ruin)

Ⓐ GATUN LOCKS

Ⓓ Chagres River

Ⓒ GATUN DAM

N

Ⓑ

GATUN LAKE

Barro Colorado Island

TOTAL PANAMA CANAL TRAFFIC

1915–1919	8,292	1960s	132,352
1920s	51,103	1970s	148,953
1930s	63,344	1980s	136,841
1940s	66,900	1990–93	55,301
1950s	96,566		

Channel Markers

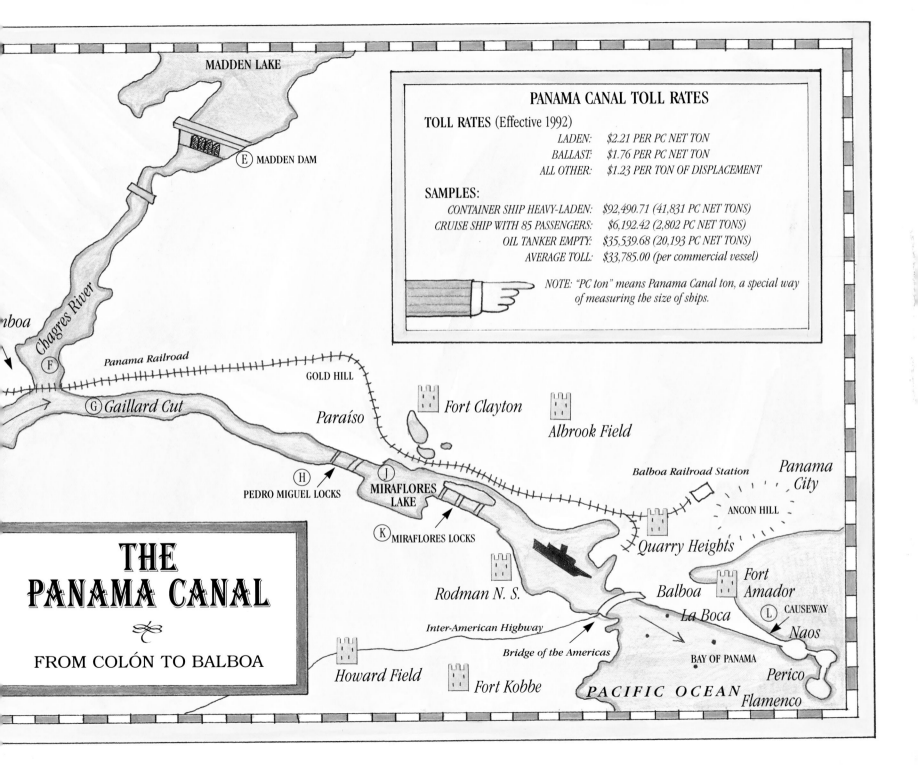

MADDEN LAKE

Ⓔ MADDEN DAM

Chagres River

Ⓕ

Panama Railroad

GOLD HILL

Ⓖ *Gaillard Cut*

Paraíso

Fort Clayton

Albrook Field

Ⓗ
PEDRO MIGUEL LOCKS

Ⓙ
MIRAFLORES LAKE

Balboa Railroad Station

Panama City

ANCON HILL

Ⓚ MIRAFLORES LOCKS

Quarry Heights

Rodman N. S.

Balboa

Fort Amador

La Boca

Ⓛ CAUSEWAY

Naos

Inter-American Highway

Bridge of the Americas

BAY OF PANAMA

THE
PANAMA CANAL

FROM COLÓN TO BALBOA

Howard Field

Fort Kobbe

PACIFIC OCEAN

Perico

Flamenco

PANAMA CANAL TOLL RATES

TOLL RATES (Effective 1992)

LADEN:	*$2.21 PER PC NET TON*
BALLAST:	*$1.76 PER PC NET TON*
ALL OTHER:	*$1.23 PER TON OF DISPLACEMENT*

SAMPLES:

CONTAINER SHIP HEAVY-LADEN:	*$92,490.71 (41,831 PC NET TONS)*
CRUISE SHIP WITH 85 PASSENGERS:	*$6,192.42 (2,802 PC NET TONS)*
OIL TANKER EMPTY:	*$35,539.68 (20,193 PC NET TONS)*
AVERAGE TOLL:	*$33,785.00 (per commercial vessel)*

NOTE: "PC ton" means Panama Canal ton, a special way of measuring the size of ships.

GOING THROUGH THE CANAL

The Canal Zone is 10 miles wide. The canal is 50 miles long from deep water in the Atlantic to deep water in the Pacific and runs northwest to southeast. It takes a ship 9 hours to travel from one end of the canal to the other. Approximately 37 ships pass through the canal every day.

When a ship approaches the canal from the Atlantic or Caribbean side, it goes through the Cristóbal breakwater into crowded Limon Bay, where it awaits its turn to enter the canal. Reservations are needed because many ships from all over the world use the canal. The ship then travels through a 6½-mile-long channel, dug through a crocodile-infested mangrove swamp, to reach Gatun Locks (A)*, the first set of locks. There the ship is raised 85 feet in a continuous flight of three steps.

Each lock is 110 feet wide by 1,000 feet long and 81 feet deep. When the ship has entered the first lock, tall steel double doors are closed, and water flows into the Apatosaurus-size concrete tub until the water level is even with the next lock chamber. Tiny locomotives called monkeys run along the sides of the lock and pull the ship into the next lock, where it is secured and water flows in again. This is repeated until the ship has been raised three times and can move into Gatun Lake (B), once the largest man-made lake in the world, which covers an area of 163.38 square miles.

Gravity is used to raise or lower the level of the water in the locks. Water flows down from the lakes into the locks. The water enters or leaves the locks through giant tunnels, or culverts, within the walls of the locks.

All the locks are twin locks, divided down the middle by narrow islands that hold the control towers and various pieces of machinery. This allows one ship to travel northwest, while another is traveling southeast at the same time.

Gatun Lake was created by the American engineers who built Gatun Dam (C) across the Chagres River (D) adjacent to Gatun Locks. Jungles, swamps, and Indian villages were flooded, and people, livestock, and wild animals had to move to higher ground. In 1935 another dam, Madden Dam (E), was built across another part of

*See map, pages 26-27

the Chagres River (F) to control the level of the canal and maintain the balance between the Atlantic and Pacific oceans.

The Chagres River's source is deep in Panama's rain forests. Panama has the most rainfall on earth, and the turbulent Chagres floods every rainy season. All the water to operate the canal comes from rain and the rain forest. The water then flows out into the oceans at either end. No water is recycled or used again.

Once the ship is on Gatun Lake, it follows a well-marked channel for 23½ miles to the entrance of the famous Gaillard Cut (G), a 500-foot-wide, 8-mile-long trench cut through the solid rock and shale of the Continental Divide. Huge crocodiles can be seen sunning themselves on rocks and shores as the ship passes by. Giant landslides here helped defeat the French and almost defeated the Americans. The Gaillard Cut (called the Culebra Cut in the French era) is named after the American engineer David Du Bose Gaillard, who was in charge of digging and blasting through that section of the canal.

At the end of the Gaillard Cut, the Pacific-bound ship enters the Pedro Miguel Locks (H), which are five-sixths of a mile long, and is lowered 31 feet in one step to Miraflores Lake (J). This is an artificial lake that separates the Pedro Miguel Locks from the Miraflores Locks (K), which are one mile long. Here the ship is lowered in two steps to sea level and exits the canal, going under the Bridge of the Americas into the Bay of Panama and the Pacific Ocean.

On the left side of the ship as it leaves the canal is the Causeway (L) that leads to the islands of Naos, Perico, and Flamenco. The Causeway was built with soil dredged from the canal and the Gaillard Cut. It protects the canal entrance from silting up, as the Pacific tides range from 12½ to 21 feet.

The Panama Railroad runs along the whole length of the canal. It was completely rebuilt and moved by U.S. engineers during the digging of the canal, when it was used to haul earth to the causeways and dams.

Within the 10-mile-wide Canal Zone are the administration buildings; control towers for the locks; hospitals, housing, schools for the canal workers and their families; U.S. forts and air force bases for defense.

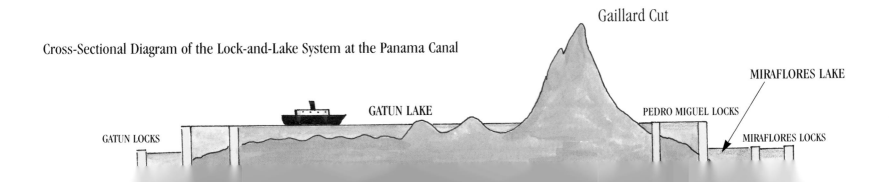

Cross-Sectional Diagram of the Lock-and-Lake System at the Panama Canal

Gaillard Cut

MIRAFLORES LAKE

GATUN LAKE

PEDRO MIGUEL LOCKS

GATUN LOCKS

MIRAFLORES LOCKS

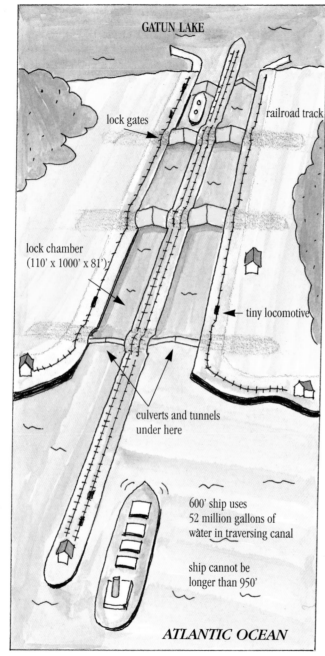

GATUN LAKE

lock gates

railroad track

lock chamber
(110' x 1000' x 81')

tiny locomotive

culverts and tunnels
under here

600' ship uses
52 million gallons of
water in traversing canal

ship cannot be
longer than 950'

ATLANTIC OCEAN

Container Ship Entering Gatun Locks

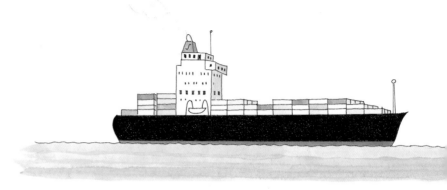

THE PANAMA CANAL TODAY

The Isthmus of Panama is where four immense ecosystems meet: the Caribbean Sea, the Pacific Ocean, North America, and South America. At one time the hemisphere's animals and plants could move across or spread through the tiny land bridge of the Isthmus. Jaguars walked north, and oak trees sprouted in the south. The Panama Canal has stopped all that.

There are two kinds of tropical forests in Panama: rain forest and dry forest. People have lived in these forests for thousands of years, but their numbers will increase greatly as Panama's population grows. New arrivals will want to chop down trees to make room for dwellings and farms and to generate income. This will put the forests in great danger and will have an impact not only on Panama but on the ecology of the whole hemisphere.

Although ships from around the world still use the

canal—carrying tons of grain, petroleum and petroleum products, containerized freight, phosphates, and ores and metals—the Panama Canal is no longer as important to the United States as it was in 1914. Only 10 to 17 percent of U.S. ships can use the canal because the locks are too short and too narrow to accommodate today's supertankers and container ships. In case of war the United States now has seven fleets in all the oceans of the world, so warships do not need to go from ocean to ocean through the canal, and the canal is now too vulnerable to be defended if attacked.

So, in accordance with the Panama Canal Treaty of 1977, by the year 2000 the U.S. government will turn over to the Republic of Panama the canal, 500 square miles of adjacent land, ten military bases, and 4,800 structures throughout the Canal Zone. All 8,500 U.S. troops will depart. But the United States will retain the right to defend the canal's neutrality forever.

Coat of Arms of the Republic of Panama
Pro Mundi Beneficio
(For the Benefit of the World)

INDEX

Page numbers in **bold** type indicate illustrations or maps.